# From Soil to Sun
# and Back Again

*Sam Razberry*

From Soil to Sky
and Back Again

ISBN: 979-8-9892133-0-6
eISBN: 979-8-9892133-1-3

Published by: Razberry Roots Publishing Co.
Cover design by: Sam Razberry
Printed in the United States of America

*Time is getting shorter*
*and there's much for you to do*
*Only ask and you will*
*get what you are needing*
*The rest is up to you*
*Plant your love and let it grow*
*Let it grow, let it grow*
*Let it blossom, let it flow*
*In the sun, the rain, the snow*
*Love is lovely, let it grow*

-Eric Clapton

*To all my sweet pollinators for helping me grow in ways I could have never imagined. You are truly what makes life beautiful.*

# Contents

## life springs forth

Ever so timid
Were my first steps into life
Springing up through frost
Into a forest full of trees
Early, but not in a hurry
A sapling of my mother's
As she was of her's
Surrounded by family and fern
Fauna and friend
Nourished through the roots of my ancestors
Kept safe and warm by the earth that held me
Enshrouded and cherished
As a brand new bloom

## youth is evergreen

My limbs swayed in harmony
To the melody of the changing seasons
Snowflakes danced around my branches
Leaving me decorated in sparkling white
Winter thawed into Spring
Whose blossoms covered my every twig
Sweetening the air with their essence
Summer sun brought salutations
With arms outstretched
Absorbing and reflecting light
To enliven my family grove
Brilliant were my leaves in Autumn
Golden, red, and fiery orange
Like the setting sun on my youth
So quickly did time fly
When I had no idea
It was passing at all

## fodder for the grove

More and more
It seems I am here to nurture others
Could it be I was created merely to serve?
As a distraction
As a purpose
As a catalyst?
I aim to please
To lighten the mood
To lessen the weight
To gather sunlight
And pass it around
Until there is none left to nourish myself
Yellow leaves once green
Litter the soft earth at my feet

## if a tree falls...

Almost imperceptible
Was the shift in the wind
I could feel the bite in the air
As the very breath of the forest
Stopped short
As the birds ceased to sing
While the fog rolled in
Lazy and foreboding
I clung to the moss and mushrooms
That sprang up where you laid
A parting gift I would have traded
To keep you standing next to me
Forever

## a duty to survive

That fall
When you came crashing
To lay still and rotting
On the forest floor
I too fell
Dropping limbs to join you
To pay homage to the life
You left behind
Not yours
But mine
Buds and leaves once vibrant
Wilted and drooped
Patches here and there
Refuse to bloom
Barren out of spite
For living while you died
Naked branches succumb to the elements
Summer and Winter
Become unbearable
Stifling heat and bitter cold
Come to collect branch after branch
Until I am a shell of myself
Raging storms take what is left of me
Chopping me off at my knees
All that is left
Is a singular leaf
Holding a seed
Begging for the strength
To leave the forest
On the next gust of wind

# make like a tree

As I cling to the stump that remains of me
I take in what is left of the forest I was born to
Fallen trees lay here and there
Covering the ground where once stood
A vast family of strong willed oaks
We are few and far between
Scattered over miles
Where we were mere feet away before
I close my eyes, and let go
Allowing the wind to pull me
Far from where I was planted

## wanderlust

Attempts to settle where I don't belong
Prove fruitless and frustrating
A barbed fence-line
The rocky bluff of a hillside
In the cracks of a city street
Time and time again
I find myself wandering
Floating on a breeze
In search of somewhere new
A comfy spot to burrow
A place to put down roots
And bloom
So it caught me by surprise
To find myself nestled
In moss that felt familiar
Near mushrooms
And a creek
That babbled
Just like you

## newly planted

The seed
When sprouting
Sees only darkness
It grows blindly through the soil
The promise of light
Guiding its very existence

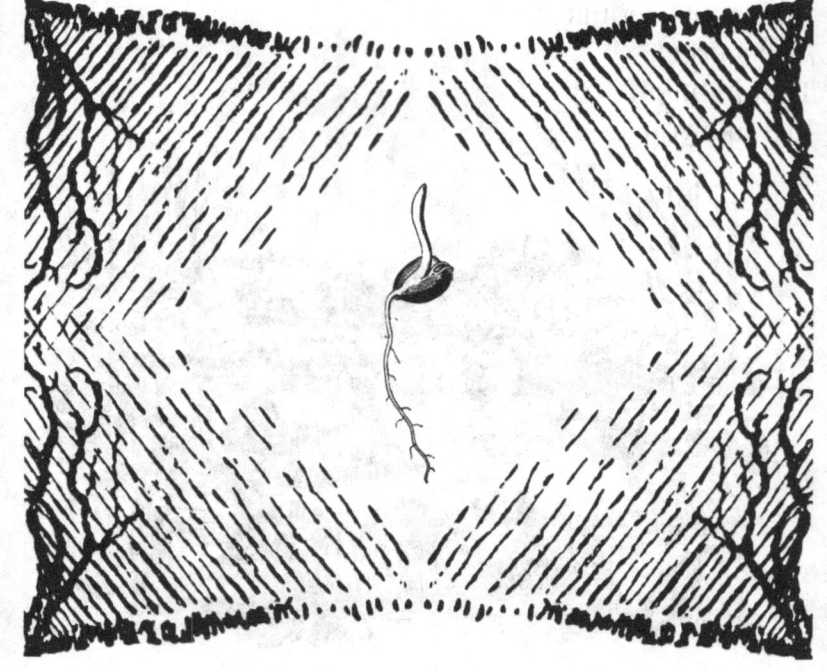

## cozy in the darkness

I found my sanctuary
Under the softest of moss beds
A cave of soil and respite
Tucked safely underground
In Mother Earth's cool embrace
Coat the walls in deepest plum
Fae light flickers in the dark
Line the shelves with knick knacks
To remind me where I'm from
Secluded from the world outside
Safe to breathe
To heal
To grow

## you belong among the wildflowers

Days turned to weeks
Then months
I spent my moments
With my head in a book
All about myself
As if in response, and reprieve
I burst through the surface
And into the springtime sun
Greeted by butterfly kisses
Tended so gently by buzzing bees
My pollen too sweet not to share
For the first time since I left home
I felt like I belonged
Right there
Among the wildflowers

## the birds & the bees: a haiku

Shake my pollen free
Cultivate my flower fields
Surround me with love

## invasive species

They were both
Beautiful
And dangerous
The kind of pairing
You're meant to nip in the bud
But I found myself captivated
By their vivid buds and blooms
And the way their vines of ivy
Held me so close
I almost didn't notice
I was suffocating
Happily dazed from a lack of space
Their embrace turned into a stranglehold
Green vines turned into legged parasites
So that when they were ripped from me
Their absence left a scar
I could have gone on forever
With them wrapped around my heart
If only I didn't wish to grow

## what lurks below

Frantically I tend to wilted flowers
Lazily molting petal by discolored petal
Dying leaves droop with exhaustion
Browning stems barely upright
I am breathless from upkeep and care
"What am I doing wrong? What could I be missing?"
I resort to endlessly watering
Unintentionally self-sabotaging
Root rot remains enshrouded
Deep below the surface of the soil
The parts of me left unseen
Tangled and hopeless for rescue
I continue to nurse the soured blooms
While the rot
Climbs ever higher
Consuming all

## grasp the nettle

I reached below the surface
I could feel where it sat
Like infection buried deep
I had to discover my way to it
Putrid, sour, and molding
Poisoning the roots around it
Rotting as it waited
For me
To see
What he had done
...
I might not make it back from here

## earthquake

I've been avoiding you.
Though we haven't spoken in years, I make an effort to
steer clear of your memory, only allowing myself
access to the vault that contains evidence of your
misgivings and dark deeds when all my walls are high
and heavily fortified.
I cannot outrun your memory, or the marks you left on
my soul.
They sprint through my subconscious mind reaching
ever upward, reminding me that beneath every stone
turned lies a hidden boulder I just hadn't considered
yet.
I was caught completely off-guard, too busy tending to
the minefield that is my history to sense you lurking
below
Just as I granted myself a moment of reprieve to relish
in the field of flowers that stood triumphant in the
wake of all my efforts, here you came.
No need to excavate as you erupted through the fresh,
new growth.
A jagged mountain and dry, cracked earth now exist
where a meadow once thrived.
Regrowth will take time and energy I barely have.
I live merely to heal, it seems.

## wither on the vine

It feels as if
I'm being pulled
Up from my roots
My hands grip soil
Dirt falls through fingers
I'm losing time
My strength is waning
I've lost my mind
My independence
My iron will
I feel I'm fading
The earth stands still
It waits for me
Stands idly by
While I decide
To Grow or Die

## return to soil

Retreat
Back to my cave
Buried deep below
Where only the earth
Knows where to find me
Above the soil
A winter storm rages
While I tend to my roots
Tendril by tender tendril
All of my nutrients
Rush to heal what is broken
Pruning the wounds left to fester
Healing my very core

## from rot comes renewal

Sacrifice what no longer serves
Let the dead and rotting parts of me
Nurture what remains
Earthworms transform
What once caused me harm
Leaving behind fertilizer
To strengthen my new roots
And hasten my growth
So that I may take on
What lies above the surface
Again
And again

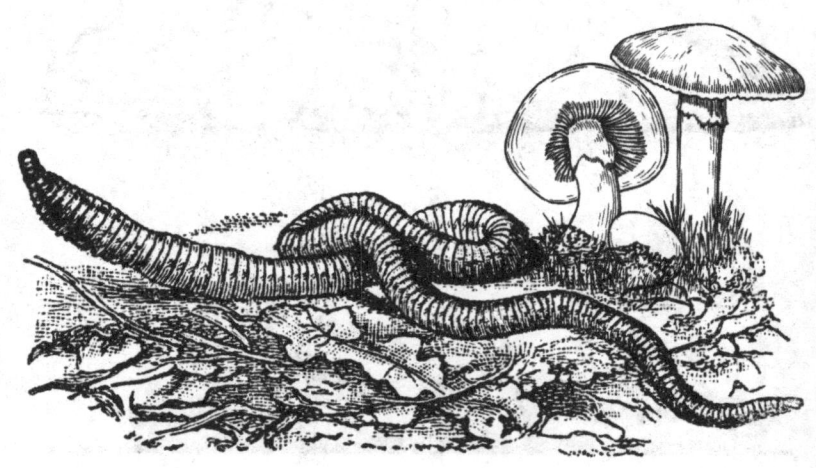

## light trickles in

Could it truly be
So dark?
Dare I...
I couldn't...
Believe that there is more?
If I could just
Press a little harder
Against the soil that surrounds me
I might just
Break through the surface
To find the sun
Warm and awaiting my arrival

# i am rooting for me

With faith and tenacity
New roots emerge
Creeping low
Into the earth
To find what needs releasing
While the seedling
Reaches ever higher
The sun shines bright on new leaves

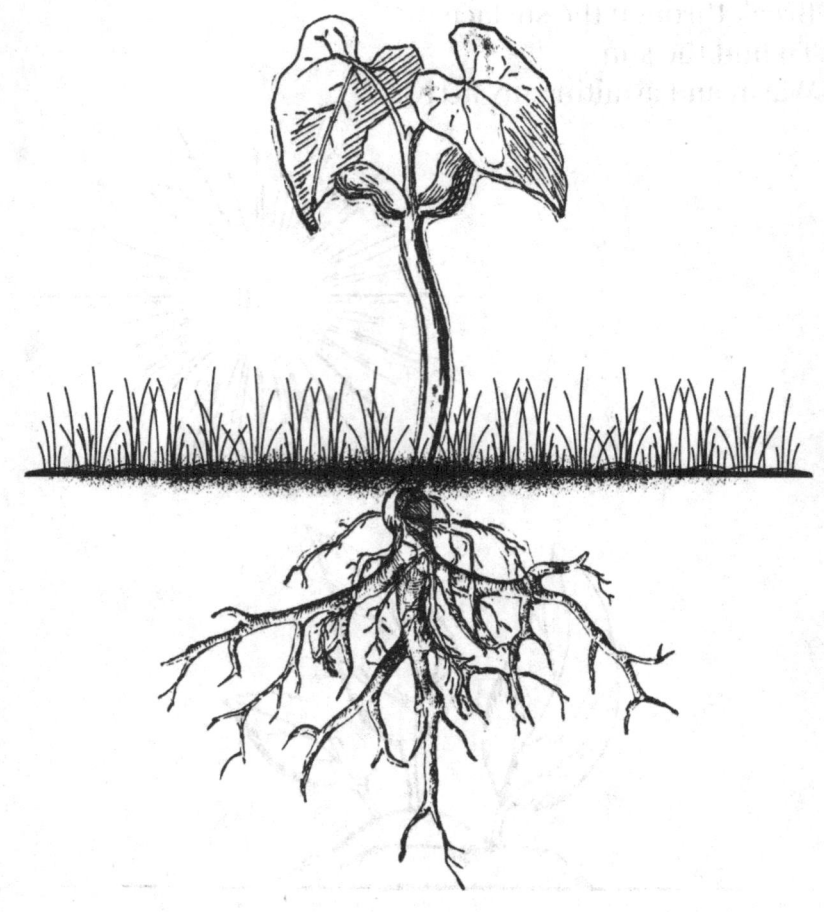

## here comes the sun

Is that the sun?
Has it come back
To shine upon my skin
Enrich my leaves, and roots, and soil
To save me from the sin
That others thrust upon me
Taking what and how they will
Picked me apart, went bit by bit
Used my vessel for their thrill
Is that the sun?
Will it reach down
And heal my damaged parts
Deliver me from evil now
Please show them that I'm yours

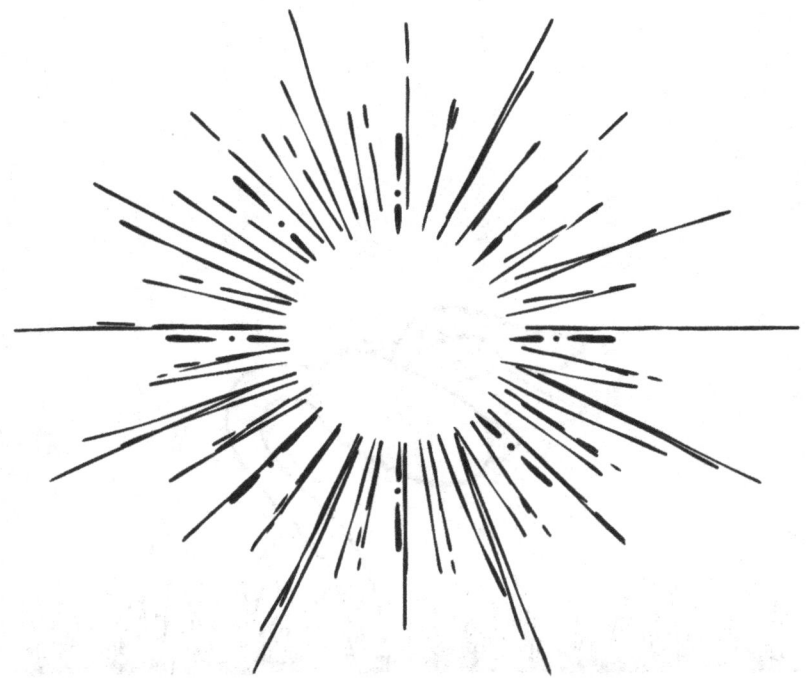

## spring's first blossom

Squinting against new light
My eyes open to take in the sun
Like new leaves unfurling
I welcome the heat, even the glare
It is uncomfortable in it's newness
As well as nourishing and soft
Gentle rays coax me ever more open
Allowing warmth to seep in
To nurture the core of me
My arms raise above my crown
A salutation to new life
A gratitude I've never known envelopes me
I am brand new, today

# thou shalt not covet thy neighbor's lawn

The grass isn't greener over the fence
It's only as green as I deem it to be
Rather than yearn for the other side's hues
I'll nurture the earth underneath my own feet

## that feeling of coming home to yourself after a long while: a series of haikus

*The knock at the door you've been waiting for*
Springtime emerges
In the cold depths of winter
So quick does it dawn

*Like the best hot chocolate you've ever had*
"Welcome home," I said
To my cold and weary bones
Love's warmth melts the ice

*That deep, satisfying breath after endlessly crying*
Into my window
Drifts a bird song full of hope
I can breathe again

*The warm embrace of the early morning sun*
Peace blooms on tree limbs
The wind recites a love song
My heart is alight

# You Are Not the Gardener You Perceive Yourself to Be

You planted me in a store-bought bag of soil, mass-
produced without care, created to do the bare
minimum, generic to its core, no expertise needed.
A one-size-fits-all solution made to cover all your
bases - or so you'd hope.
I am not a generic plant, not the shrinking violet of
your dreams, but you knew that when you picked me
out.
Much like a succulent, I require patience and a deeper
understanding of what lifts me up, what rots my roots,
and how best to love me for my soul to shine; for my
heart to feel safe to unpin its petals, and bloom.
You operated with little regard to my needs.
Instead of a gentle, steady mist, you waterboarded me
with attention and what I mistook for love, only to
leave me parched and wilting when you withdrew
all together.
You pruned the parts of me that didn't serve you until I
was something different entirely.
Sat alone on a shelf, I spent countless nights wishing to
be more than a trophy in your case.
With enough mistreatment I grew spines, barbed and
sharp, primed for asserting my needs, my boundaries.
You'd curse me when you pricked your finger, but it
was you who reached out to poke what could stab you
back.
You led me down the garden path, but I found my way
back home.
Like a lotus flower navigating the murky depths, I grew
blindly with only my faith in myself to sustain my
journey.

Reaching ever higher I bloomed, wholly outgrowing you, and the container you chose for me.
The flower crown atop my head pays tribute and gratitude to the love with which I water myself. No longer bound to pots, I have made my home under the sun.
Grounding myself into the earth as I reach toward the sky in celebration for all I have witnessed.
I am growth personified.

# barking up the wrong tree

I cannot be
Your giving tree
Can't give and give
Until I'm gone
Can't let you chop
Away at me
To sacrifice
Myself feels wrong

I cannot be
The one you task
With saving you
From your abuse
Can't be the space
You rest your axe
With sharpened words
For cutting through

I cannot be
Your saving grace
Can't put myself
Up on a shelf
I cannot breathe
Life into you
While calling out
To ask for help

I cannot be
Your giving tree
Can't give and give
Until I'm gone
I'll break away
And fly on free
A southern wind
Carries me home

## companion planting

There we grow
Sprouting
Breaking through hard earth
Compact and impossible as bedrock
There we thrive
Despite winter frost and torrential rain
To witness you is an honor
Let me tend to your leaves while you support my stems
I will help you soften your soil
And gently untangle your roots when you feel bound
With understanding and compassion
For the circumstances in which we were planted
Together we blossom
In sun and in storms
Season after season
We bloom

# a bed of roses

Little growth
Passive growth
Quiet growth
Is just
Big
Profound
Loud growth
And respite
In disguise

## let love grow

I have known all manifestation of caring
There are those who left me parched
Wrinkling and wilting
In the sun's relentless gaze
Others, who's nurturing was obligatory
Who would water me incessantly
And blame me when I drowned
Broken reeds and tarnished expectations
Kept me clutching at straws
To survive, never thrive
Then came those with their green thumbs
Who gently pried me from my undersized pot
And swaddled me in loam rich in nutrients
That nourished my wounded roots
Bringing me to bloom like never before
This is how love blossoms

## reclamation

Alone in a field
Sits the house that built me
Decrepit and falling inward
It exists solely to be broken down
Sunlight plays through a roof filled with holes
Weaving vines with swirling tendrils
Wrap lovingly around beam and board
The wild and warring parts of me
Span the small space that I once embodied
Until my true nature takes over
Reclaiming what is mine

## growing & sowing

I wish to inspire growth beyond measure
To bask in love's natural cycles
And breathe deep the scent of sweet honeysuckle
As it blooms wild and free
Let me be a vessel of hope, humility, and grace
To lift the spirits of the wilted and weary
Send the birds and bees
To carry my seeds to barren fields
So my love may bloom all over

# Books By This Author

## Being Human: You Signed Up For This

Being Human: You Signed Up For This is a journal written from the perspective of a spiritual being living a human existence. It is a raw and honest depiction of what it is like to traverse through life in all its complexities; from unearthing trauma and heartache, to finding the will to persevere through our darkest moments, survive and finally thrive. A deep dive into fear and anguish evolves into an inspiring journey of self-love and acceptance. Sometimes it takes digging into the hurt parts of ourselves to heal old wounds, and that approach is at the forefront of this author's quest to understand what it is truly like Being Human.

# Acknowledgements

Well, friends, here we are again. Another book published, another lengthy acknowledgements section. This time, since I mentioned all my loves in my first book's acknowledgements page(s), I thought I would go a different route, and thank those who inspired several poems in this book. If not for my experiences loving (and occasionally losing) them, over half of these poems would cease to be. Whether you are present for a lifetime or a season, I love you for your contribution to my life.

"If a Tree Falls" & "A Duty to Survive": Life would have severely lacked meaning without the man who I humbly believe I inherited most of my most lovable traits from. My Papa (read: pawpaw) was the first loss I ever experienced that shook me to my very core. It's been over twenty years, but there are still days where his absence is felt as strongly as the day he passed. There is not an accomplishment, a great day, a terrible day, or a worst moment that goes by without his energy coming forward to encourage me onward.

Even in death, his love is all-encompassing. Thank you endlessly, Papa, for the Nerds, for the catch-and-release lizards, for teaching me compassion and how to shuffle cards, for showing me what a loving man truly embodied, for the midnight snacks shared at the kitchen table, and so so much more. I will love you even when I return to stardust.

"Wanderlust": It may seem silly to others, but sometimes a place feels like family. Leaving Texas (specifically Houston) was something I never thought I would do. Terrible politics and questionable population aside, the state itself is a piece of me that I cherish. The winding roads, incredible sunsets, the Houston skyline, the ocean waves crashing against the shoreline under the Galveston seawall... There is a beauty to all of it that was unmatched. Then, I left out of desperation, impulsivity, and a yearning for something unknown. I wandered my way to middle Tennessee, among hills, trees, and enough civilization and creature comforts to mimic how I felt in Houston. For the first time since I left Texas in my rearview, I felt like I was home. Bless these beautiful spaces I have had the honor to love so dearly.

"Invasive Species", "Earthquake", "You are not the gardener...", & "Barking Up the Wrong Tree": These go out to those that tore through the tender parts of me, who acted as catalysts for growth, encouraging me in their roundabout way to show up for myself - no matter what. If not for loving you and losing you, for walking away or picking up the pieces of me after you left, I would not know the sheer amount of strength I possess just for rehabilitating myself. So, thank you, for leaving your mark on my life, if only for the irreplaceable lessons, and the bangers you inspired me to write. Here's hoping you're out there growing, too.

"Companion Planting": You know who you are. Thank you to the loves that have enriched my life in ways I could never repay, but I will sure strive to match – like the energy we exchange. Our presence in each other's life is symbiotic, mutually beneficial and loving, caring, and compassionate. Thank you for growing alongside me. Thank you for holding space when I need it, and for closing the gap when I need to be held. I am eternally grateful to experience life with all of you by my side, and to be a witness to your own growing seasons. It is an honor and a privilege to be a love in your life.

As always, thank you to myself. To all the versions of me that got me here. To the parts of me that cried out for help. To my heart for remaining open and willing to heal over and over again. Looking back over the last five years, I am in awe of the amount of love I showed myself. It was always second nature to love others. Loving myself, on the other hand, was a different story. There was judgement, shame, and guilt for self-abandoning and subjecting others to the worst parts of me. There were so many reasons – in my mind – to hate myself, that the idea of loving myself seemed far out of my reach. It wasn't until I began shedding what didn't serve me that I started to feel the slightest tug from deep within my being. A muffled thrumming of energy pounding against its confines where my body had hidden it away until I was ready for it to be revealed. The "Big Bad" I called it. Once my body and mind decided I was fit to receive the images and memories it had held from me, I had no choice but to love myself through it or disappear into nothingness.

My brain plagued me with flashbacks every minute of every day for months. I was terrified to leave my safe spaces and people. I couldn't even use the bathroom without leaving the door open, or having someone come with me, even one of my dogs would do. I had breakdowns from intense flashbacks that left me in the fetal position on the floor of the shower. Everything was a trigger point. It took a willingness to dig into all those hurt parts of me, with intentional, consistent effort to be gentle and compassionate with myself. Therapy, meds, yoga, hundreds of salt baths, reassurance from my closest loves, releasing those whose journeys were no longer parallel to my own, more therapy, ample self-awareness, and introspection all led the charge to shed light on all my shadows. All those rotten, unkempt parts of me were tended to with love and grace until flowers grew where there was once decay. I could never thank my Self enough for getting me through one of the hardest parts of my journey, but I will continue to show up and show out for my healing, and make all those versions of me proud.

So here is to all of you - myself included - who were written into my story. May your own journeys be lined with fields of wildflowers, and love beyond measure. See you in the next chapter...